20 Minute GUIDE To The SIKH FAITH

GIAN SINGH SANDHU

20 Minute Guide To The SIKH FAITH

Gian Singh Sandhu
gianssandhu@gmail.com

Other books by the author:

Angahe Raah *(2019), (Punjabi translation of An Uncommon Road). Unistar Books, Chandigarh, India.*

An Uncommon Road *: How Canadian Sikhs Struggled Out of the Fringes and into the Mainstream (2018). Echo Storytelling Agency, Vancouver, Canada.*

Contributions to other books :

Guru Nanak's Benediction May You Be Displaced! *(2019) In Dr. Gurvinder Singh (Ed.),* ***Guru Nanak Darshan :*** *Philosophy of Guru Nanak (pp. 114-119). Sri Guru Singh Sabha, Surrey, B.C.*

Odysseys of a Spiritual Messenger *(2019) In Dr. Gurnam Singh Sanghera, (Ed.),* ***Guru Nanak :*** *Revealer of Truth (pp. 89-120). India Cultural Centre of Canada, Richmond, B.C.*

Guru Nanak's Relative and Absolute Truth *(2019) In Dr. Gurnam Singh Sanghera, (Ed.),* **Guru Nanak Sahib***: Jagat Guru – Founder of New World Order (pp. 73-84). Akali Singh Sikh Society, Vancouver, B.C.*

20 Minute Guide to the Sikh Faith

by

Gian Singh Sandhu

First Edition: 2020

ISBN: 978-1-7772523-0-4 (Canada)

1. Sikhi 2. Sikhism 3. Sikh History 4. Sikh Gurdwara 5. Sikh Rehat Maryada 5. Sikh Marriage Ceremony 7. Guru Granth Sahib 8. Sikh Articles of Faith. 9. Title

Published by

BHALAEE FOUNDATION
Surrey, B.C. Canada
604-341-2755

Printed In India

Dedicated
To
Guru Nanak Sahib's
550th
Commemoration Anniversary

TABLE OF CONTENTS

FOREWORD

Sikh religion, despite being relatively new, is the fifth-largest living religion of the world. It is deeply rooted in the spiritual and historical experiences of Guru Nanak (1469-1539). A close examination of Guru Nanak's writing, particularly spiritual hymns, make it abundantly clear that the lack of spirituality, immoral behaviour, and caste-based social order were not acceptable to him. He was determined to convey that there is only "One Divine Being," who loves all and can be realized equally by everyone, notwithstanding gender or social status. His spiritual, poetic utterances, sung in nineteen melodies, established a distinct faith and provided a new social order, afresh with ideological alternatives aimed at spiritual regeneration and social reconstruction of which truthful living, equality, equity, and justice were the fundamental values.

Five hundred years ago, in the midst of a highly patriarchal society, Guru Nanak took a stand for the empowerment of women and gender equality. The uniqueness of Sikh spirituality lies in the fact that it neither subscribes to otherworldliness nor confines itself to liberation at the individual level. It is a congregational religion that takes care of both worlds, *Deen* (spiritual) and *Duniya* (secular), in equal measure. It is all-inclusive and holistic in its approach towards the world and the concerns of human life. Sikhism is a life affirmative and holistic religion that not only focuses on a family and householder lifestyle but also believes in the welfare of humanity. Its' mission is to eradicate evil and injustice from all walks of life. Epistemologically speaking, it was a radical departure from the Indian religious tradition. It was a quantum leap in Indian spirituality as it broke the barriers of caste and threw open the doors for liberation. It was a social and religious revolution.

The present study, *20 Minute Guide to the Sikh Faith,* has been written with an avowed objective to educate young Sikhs and introduce the faith to non-Sikhs. The author discusses the origin and development of Sikhism very briefly and takes into account the epoch-making events that left an indelible imprint on the psyche and history of the Sikhs. He dwells upon the most significant beliefs and practices, namely the Sikh Scripture, the institution of Gurdwara, the Sikh code of conduct, Five Ks (five articles of Sikh faith), rites of passage, the Sikh festivals, etc. in a very cogent and lucid style. Besides the table of dates relating to the lives of Sikh Gurus, the author has very wisely given the gist of hymns that are recited to solemnize the Sikh marriage ceremony known as *Anand Karaj*. Simply put, it serves the purpose of reminding the newly wedded couple of their duties and commitment towards each other and society as well. Though the author is very candid and humble in his claim that "It is by no means a comprehensive or categorical" treatise, yet he has succeeded in his objective to fulfill the reader's quest to know more about Sikhism. I appreciate it very much and congratulate S. Gian Singh Sandhu for this accomplishment.

Professor (Dr.) Balwant Singh Dhillon
Formerly Founder Director
Centre for Studies in Sri Guru Granth Sahib
Guru Nanak Dev University
Amritsar - 143005

INTRODUCTION

This guidebook is intended to provide readers with a brief glimpse into Sikh[1] values, beliefs, practices, and traditions. It is by no means comprehensive or categorical. Like any other faith group, Sikhs are not homogeneous ethnically or in terms of how they each interpret their Guru's teachings and choose to apply them to their own lives. However, observant Sikhs share much in common, starting with a firm belief in the spiritual teachings compiled in the *Sri Guru Granth Sahib,*[2] the Sikh Scripture. Thus, much of this book will focus on those teachings while also touching on the practices of Sikhs that have developed since the beginning of the Guru's times and are designed to put those teachings into action.

Guru Nanak is widely considered to be one of the most influential religious teachers of all time. He was a radical socio-religious thinker who fearlessly challenged existing social norms. Based on his profound divine experience, and dialogue with different faith-based leaders throughout

---

[1] The word "Sikh" is pronounced with the short "i" sound, as in "pick".

[2] Prefix 'Sri' and suffix 'Sahib' are honorific titles added to all Gurus' names.

India and the Middle East, he weaved spiritual thought into a unique philosophy and distinct identity that has left an indelible imprint on this world. *Sikhi*[3] (Sikh religion) is a monotheistic faith, and in that respect, it is similar to other world religions. However, there are critical differences between Sikhi and other religions, which will become evident as you read this book. One of its unique features is the Sikh concept of the saint-soldier *(sant-sapahi)* – a brave individual who balances the quest for personal enlightenment with social activism.

I invite you to join me as we briefly explore Sikh philosophy, institutions, values, and practices – in short, 'the Sikh way of life.' Whether you are hoping to learn more about your Sikh heritage, or are simply curious about your next-door neighbour, I hope this book helps you on your quest for knowledge.

Gian Singh Sandhu
Surrey, British Columbia, Canada
gianssandhu@gmail.com

---

[3] The word "Sikhi" is pronounced "Sikhee". This is how most Sikhs refer to their faith.

1. HISTORY

Our journey begins in 1469 CE in the village of 'Rai Bhoe Di Talwandi,' where Guru Nanak, the founder of the Sikh faith, was born. The village was renamed in his honour and is now known as Nankana and is located in Punjab, [4] Pakistan, about 65 kilometers from Lahore.

The decades surrounding Guru Nanak's birth were a time of great social and religious upheaval in India and, indeed, the world. Columbus had only recently 'discovered' the Americas. Nicolaus Copernicus was working on his seminal theory that the Sun and not the Earth was at the centre of our solar system. And Martin Luther was on the cusp of starting the Protestant Reformation. Closer to home, Guru Nanak was an eyewitness to the Mughal invasions of India and wrote about the atrocities perpetrated on the

[4] Punjab is pronounced "pan-ja-b." It literally means the land of five (panj) rivers (ab). After the partition of India in 1947, the Punjab province of British India was split between India and Pakistan.

people of the Indian subcontinent by the invading forces.

All of these events helped form and shape Guru Nanak's vision of creating a community of socially responsible and spiritually aware individuals. He was a visionary, centuries ahead of his time. During a period when women were treated as mere chattels and considered sub-human, he advocated against female infanticide, widow burning *(sati)*[5], and the veiling of women's faces. He maintained that all religions were equal and sought to unify people of different faiths. Guru Nanak encouraged a radical transformation in how individuals lived their life, promoting self-awareness and truthful living - which are integral to the Sikh path.

Guru Nanak's life has been documented and passed on to succeeding generations through *Janamsakhis,* which chronicle the development of his thought and revolution against the status quo. One such *Janamsakhi* recounts how, at the age of nine, Guru Nanak refused to wear the *janeu,* a sacred religious thread worn by Hindu males as their initiation into the religious order and to

[5] The Indian practice of 'sati,", where widows were compelled to immolate themselves on their husbands' funeral pyres.

distinguish themselves from other (lower) castes. He did not want to reinforce social and gender disparity. He proclaimed that people should be known for their qualities and their deeds, rather than symbolic thread, rituals, or blind faith.

Towards the end of the fifteenth century, Guru Nanak had a profound spiritual experience that led to his vision of the true nature of human existence and our relationship with the Divine Creator. He saw the Creator as a benevolent and' wondrous teacher' (*Waheguru*[6]), accessible to all (*sarb-sanjha*), regardless of gender, race, ethnicity, or religious belief. He viewed himself as a student (the literal translation for the word *"Sikh"*) of this wondrous teacher. Guru Nanak challenged the prevalent socio-religious practices and declared that anyone could connect with Waheguru anytime and anywhere, without any rituals or needing an intermediary.

According to Guru Nanak, Waheguru could be experienced by earning an honest living (*kirat karna*); embarking on a quest for internal purity through meditation (*naam japna*); and sharing

---

[6] Waheguru: pronounced "wha-hey-guru," is the most commonly used Sikh name for the Divine Creator. It may also be spelled 'vahiguru'.

one's earnings with others, particularly the needy (*vand chhakna*). These three principles have become the pillars of the Sikh way of life. They require a real and practical commitment to life and its ethical obligations. If practiced daily, Guru Nanak believed that they would lead to a holistic and fulfilling life, leading one to become a spiritually aware and socially responsible person.

Guru Nanak travelled extensively, on foot and sea, throughout India and the Middle East, spreading his message of the Creator and empowering humans to rise above the temptations of lust (*kaam*), anger (*krodh*), greed (*lobh*), attachment (*moh*), and ego (*ahankaar*). Those that followed his teachings became known as Sikhs.

Following four odysseys undertaken over twenty plus years, Guru Nanak settled with his wife and two children in the village of Kartarpur. He eventually felt the need to pass on the torch of his mission and chose a successor. There were nine successive gurus following Guru Nanak. Over a period of 200 years, each expounded upon and reinforced Guru Nanak's spiritual teachings and helped develop institutions to put these teachings into practice. These include the sangat (devout congregation), *gurdwara* (Sikh place of worship);

langar (community kitchen), *pangat* (sitting together and dining without any distinction of social status), and *kirtan* (singing of devotional hymns).

The simplicity and beauty of Guru Nanak's message empowered the downtrodden and emboldened them to challenge the status quo. As more people embraced the Sikh way of life, the Sikhs were increasingly viewed as a threat to the existing social structure and became targets of persecution by the state.

Guru Arjan, the fifth Sikh guru, was tortured and martyred for his refusal to bow to the demands of the Mughal Emperor Jahangir. The sixth Guru, Guru Hargobind, was imprisoned for years for also challenging the Emperor. Guru Teg Bahadur, the ninth Guru, was martyred for standing up for the freedom of Hindus to practice their faith free of interference and intimidation by the Mughal rulers.

Persecution of Sikhs continued, and they were forced to fight back and defend themselves under the leadership of the tenth Guru, Guru Gobind Singh. One of Guru Gobind Singh's generals was a highly regarded woman named Mata Bhag Kaur, who led Sikh soldiers in the battle against the Mughals in 1705 CE. Guru Gobind Singh was fatally stabbed by a Mughal mercenary. His *Joti Jot* (immersion in Eternal Light) occurred in 1708 CE and was preceded by the martyrdom of all four of his children, the older two dying in battle, and the younger two [7] entombed alive by the Mughal rulers for refusing to give up their faith.

Guru Gobind Singh was the last Guru in human form for the Sikhs. Before *Joti Jot,* he proclaimed the *Sri Guru Granth Sahib* (the Sikh Scripture) as the eternal Guru to whom Sikhs should turn for spiritual guidance. He bestowed the temporal authority for the conduct of Sikh affairs, on the *Khalsa Panth* (the collective body of Sikhs who accept *Amrit*, the initiation ceremony for a practicing Sikh). With a shared destiny and vision, and guided by the Scripture, the Sikh community has remained united following Guru Gobind Singh Joti Jot.

[7] The older two sons Baba Ajit Singh and Baba Jujhar Singh were 18 and 14 years old respectively, and the younger sons Baba Zorawar Singh and Baba Fateh Singh were just 9 and 7 years old.

Baba[8] Banda Singh Bahadur (1670-1716), who was initiated into Sikh faith by Guru Gobind Singh at Nanded (central India), became a devout Sikh and renowned warrior. In September 1708 CE, with Guru Gobind Singh's blessing, he left for Punjab and raised a Sikh army to battle against cruel Mughal oppression. In the following two years, he managed to carve out a sovereign Sikh state in Northern India. This was the beginning of the downfall of the Mughal empire. Following Banda Singh Bahadur's barbaric execution in Delhi in 1716 CE, the first Sikh State fell apart. The Mughal governors of Punjab followed a relentless policy to exterminate the Sikhs as a religious community. Sikhs were hunted like wild beasts, imprisoned, and executed publicly in the markets of Lahore.

The persecution of Sikhs led to the battle known as the *Wadda Ghalughara* (major holocaust). On February 5, 1762, it was estimated that 30,000 Sikhs were killed (martyred) in battle in one day. Instead of becoming demoralized, the Sikhs showed true grit, and the disparate

---

[8] *Baba* means grandfather, or wise elder, it is an honorific used to refer to someone who is deeply respected for their knowledge and leadership, regardless of their age. The female term is *Bibi*.

independent misls (confederacies) eventually amalgamated to create the Sikh *raaj* (Empire) under the leadership of *Maharaja* (head king) Ranjit Singh in 1799 CE.

Maharaja Ranjit Singh's empire extended from the Khyber Pass in the west (northwest frontier province of Pakistan), the river Satluj in the east, Mithankot in the south, and Kashmir in the north. Though his adherence to Sikh teachings in his personal life is often questioned, Ranjit Singh was appropriately regarded as a fair and impartial ruler. In Ranjit Singh's kingdom, all faiths were given equal opportunity, and capital punishment was abolished. He appointed Sikhs, Muslims, Hindus, Christians, and people of other faiths to authoritative positions in his administration. Indeed, his army had generals from France, Italy, and America.

Having conquered the rest of India some fifty years earlier, the British saw it opportune to annex what remained of Ranjit Singh's empire in 1849 CE, merely ten years after his death. However, it was an uneasy reign, with many Indians, including Sikhs, openly rejecting British rule.

The movement to be free of British rule was ultimately successful. In 1947 CE, the people of

India gained independence from the British, but not before losing millions of lives during Partition. The British agreed to split the country into three, creating the Muslim majority countries of East and West Pakistan and the Hindu majority country of India.

The Sikhs, who had their own empire before British occupation of it and had lost the most lives freeing India, ended up being short-changed during Partition. Relying on promises made by the Indian political leaders (Jawaharlal Nehru[9] and Mohandas Karamchand Gandhi) that their distinct identity would be protected in a newly independent India, the Sikhs opted not to seek an independent country of their own. Sadly, Nehru and Gandhi failed to keep their word. This betrayal of the Sikh community led Sikhs to face many needless challenges in post-colonial India.

Modern Indian history has been marked by border disputes with Pakistan and China, as well as internal sectarian conflict as religious minorities (such as Christians, Sikhs, and

---

[9] "The brave Sikhs of Punjab are entitled to special consideration," vowed Nehru, a year before India was granted independence and he became the nation's first prime minister. "I see nothing wrong in an area and a set-up in the North wherein the Sikhs can also experience the glow of freedom," reported The Statesman – July 6, 1946.

Muslims) seek to protect their own identities. For the Sikhs, this came to a head in 1984 CE, when the government of India launched a full-fledged military assault (codenamed '*Operation Blue Star*') against the Sikhs who were advocating for greater rights for all states (including Punjab).

Operation Blue Star resulted in the loss of thousands of innocent lives. The Indian government's orchestrated attack on *Darbar Sahib* (Golden Temple), the destruction of the *Akal Takhat Sahib* (seat of Sikh temporal authority) and Sikh archives, and a simultaneous attack on thirty-eight other historical gurdwaras reverberated around the Sikh diaspora. This direct attack on Sikh places of worship has been the focal point of continuous Sikh disillusionment with post-colonial India.

Though some Sikhs then favoured the creation of a distinct state where Sikhs could live, flourish, and experience the glow of freedom, Sikhs remain a vital part of India. Moreover, the Sikh diaspora is genuinely global. Today, there are more than 28 million Sikhs in the world, with the most significant numbers outside of India living in Canada, Great Britain, the United States, Australia, New Zealand, and Malaysia.

2. SIKH GREETINGS

Two greetings are commonly used amongst Sikhs:

1. *Waheguru Ji Ka Khalsa Waheguru Ji Ki Fateh,* meaning “Khalsa (sovereign) belongs to the Creator and victory belongs to the Creator.” At the time of the establishment of the Sikh initiation *(Amrit)* ceremony in 1699 CE, Guru Gobind Singh, the tenth Sikh Guru, invoked all Sikhs to greet each other with this greeting. It is most commonly used amongst initiated Sikhs.
2. *Sat Sri Akal* - which is the most common greeting, is the second part of the full Sikh slogan or Jaikara (call to victory, triumph or exultation). The full slogan is *“Bole So Nihal,* Sat *Sri Akal,”* meaning “Whoever utters this phrase shall be happy and blessed; eternal is the Great Timeless Divine.” This slogan was introduced during Guru Gobind Singh time.

Contrary to customary English greetings, which reflect specific occasions or times of day, the Sikh greeting is the same for all times, occasions, and events.

3. THE SIKH GURUS

The word "guru" refers to a spiritual teacher, and can be defined as the "deliverer from darkness (ignorance) to light (enlightenment)." The term "Sikh" is defined as a student and a seeker of truth. Thus, the Gurus taught Sikhs how to move from darkness to light, from ignorance to enlightenment, from fear to confidence, from hate to love, and from despair to hope.

While Sikhs believe that the guidance of the Guru is essential to one's spiritual enlightenment, the Sikh religion rejects the notion that the human Guru is a mediator between the disciple and *Waheguru*. Rather, Guru Nanak emphasized a personal and direct relationship with the Divine. The Guru's role is to reveal the way to establish that relationship but never to come between the seeker and *Waheguru*.

The Gurus' names and their period of Guruship are listed below :

The Gurus and Guruship Period

Name	Life span	Guruship period(CE)
Guru Nanak Sahib	1469-1539	1469-1539
Guru Angad Sahib	1504-1552	1539-1552
Guru Amardas Sahib	1479-1574	1552-1574
Guru Ramdas Sahib	1534-1581	1574-1581
Guru Arjan Sahib	1563-1606	1581-1606
Guru Hargobind Sahib	1595-1644	1606-1644
Guru Har Rai Sahib	1630-1661	1644-1661
Guru Harkrishan Sahib	1656-1664	1661-1664
Guru Teg Bahadur Sahib	1621-1675	1664-1675
Guru Gobind Singh Sahib	1666-1708	1675-1708
Sri Guru Granth Sahib Ji		1708 onwards

The most common prefix, Sri, is a title of respect. Sikhs also use the suffixes Ji and Sahib or Saheb and sometimes the combination of Sahib Ji after a name or title. Using these honorifics for Sikh Gurus is similar to Christians using Lord or Saviour for Jesus and Orthodox Jews feeling so much awe in God that they write this word only as G-d, without ever spelling it out entirely.

4. SRI GURU GRANTH SAHIB

Sri Guru Nanak Sahib expressed his teachings through his profoundly moving and exquisitely written *Gurbani* (divine utterances). These spiritual writings form the basis of the Sikh Scripture. In addition to Guru Nanak, five other Sikh Gurus also expressed their spiritual ideology in the form of hymns.

Guru Arjan compiled the very first formulation of the Sikh Scriptures, known as the *Aad Granth* (the primal Scripture). In addition to his own writings and those of his predecessors, Guru Arjan included the spiritual writings of saints and devotees from other faiths and diverse social backgrounds whose thinking was congruent with Guru Nanak's teachings.

The inclusion of the teachings of non-Sikhs in the Sikh Scripture is an extraordinary display of openness that is the hallmark of Sikh faith. It drives home the Sikh view that each religion is equal, and at its core, teaches the same fundamental values. When Sikhs bow to their Scripture, they are bowing not only to the teachings of the Sikh Gurus, but also the compositions of other spiritually enlightened individuals who professed other faiths.

Guru Gobind Singh canonized the final version of the Sikh Scripture, which is in use today. Included in it were the writings of Guru Teg Bahadur. Though a gifted poet himself, Guru Gobind Singh in his humbleness, did not include his own writings. He named the Sikh Scripture the Guru Granth. Sikhs add 'Sri' before Guru Granth and 'Sahib' after, as a title of reverence. Before his *Joti Jot* in 1708 CE, Guru Gobind Singh proclaimed the Sri Guru Granth Sahib as the eternal Guru of the Sikhs, to which Sikhs could turn for spiritual guidance. He also declared that the Panj Pyare (any five initiated and practicing Sikhs) could constitute a decision-making body and provide guidance in secular matters, such as leadership in social issues or assisting with interpretation of the Gurus' teachings.

Sri Guru Granth Sahib is a 1,430-page volume written in *Gurmukhi* (Punjabi script popularized by the Gurus). Virtually all of the compilations are set to musical modes (*raags*). Similar to French, Punjabi incorporates the use of the masculine and feminine tense. Though all the gurus were male, the Sikh Scripture is written in the feminine tense, reflecting the Gurus' belief that each of our souls, regardless of gender, is best expressed as feminine energy.

Guru Nanak's vision was to reveal the true nature of the Divine and foster the creation of an all-inclusive and egalitarian society. The very first spiritual composition *(sabd)* in the Sri Guru Granth Sahib (known as the *mool mantar, or* the cardinal statement) sets out the mission statement for every Sikh. It captures Guru Nanak's vision of the Ultimate Divine Source, and by extension, of the Self:

> ***Ek Onkaar*** – *there is one eternal being that is all-embracing*
> ***Satnam*** – *whose name is 'the one that exists'*
> ***Karta*** – *the Creator of the Universe*
> ***Purakh*** – *the cosmic consciousness which permeates through all of creation*
> ***Nirbhau*** – *that which has no fear*
> ***Nirvair*** – *that which has no enmity*
> ***Akal moorat*** – *that form which is not bound by time*
> ***Ajooni*** – *that which is unborn*
> ***Saibhang*** – *that which came into existence on its own*
> ***Gur parsad*** – *that which can be realized with the grace of the true Guru*

5. GURDWARA

The gurdwara (literally the Guru's door or gateway to the Guru) is the hub of the Sikh community, spirituality, and culture. It is a place where Sikhs gather to meditate, congregate, celebrate, and commemorate. A gurdwara is open to all; each gurdwara is built with four doors yet only one entranceway, signifying that people from all four corners of the Earth, and of all faiths, castes, and genders, are welcome, and enter as equals. In some countries having four doors may be constrained due to land or zoning by-laws.

A gurdwara is easily recognizable from afar, distinguishable by a '*Nishan Sahib*' (a long pole with the Sikh flag on it) present outside every gurdwara. The flag is triangular and usually saffron-colored (though some flags may be blue). At the centre is the *khanda* – the symbol of Sikhi. The design of the khanda reflects some of the core concepts that govern Sikh teachings. The name "khanda" is actually derived from the double-edged sword in the center, which is also called a khanda. The central sword is meant to be a metaphor for one's spiritual journey; the sharp edges cleaving truth from falsehood. The circle around the khanda is called the *chakar.* It represents the Eternal Divine, with no beginning and no end.[10] The two curved outer swords of the *khanda* are the swords of '*Piri*' (spiritual power) and '*Miri*' (temporal power). They remind a Sikh of her or his duty to strive for balance in life by placing equal value on spiritual aspirations and fulfilling one's social obligations.

The typical design of a gurdwara comprises a central dome on the rooftop, with smaller domes at the corners. The design is not prescribed. If the collective economic well-being of devotees at any given place does not permit this costly construction, then appropriate adjustments are made to the buildings of worship. The emphasis

Akali Singh Sikh Society, Vancouver, BC

[10] In the words of Sri Guru Nanak Sahib, *aad sach, jugaad sach, hai bhi sach, Nanak hosi bhi sach* – that which existed in the primal beginning, that which existed through the ages, that which exists here and now, oh Nanak, that which will exist forever.

is not on the building but on the purpose of its usage.

The most famous gurdwara is Darbar Sahib, also referred to as Harmandar Sahib in Amritsar, India. In the western world, it is commonly known as the "Golden Temple."It came by this nickname after Maharaja Ranjit Singh gilded it with nearly a ton of gold. Darbar Sahib was constructed under the supervision of Guru Arjan, the fifth Guru. In explicit acknowledgement of the concept of only ONE spiritual path leading to the Divine, Guru Arjan invited a Muslim Sufi saint (Sain[11] Mian Mir) to lay the foundation stone for Darbar Sahib. The gurdwara lies in the centre of a massive complex, surrounded by a rectangular pool of water. *Akal Takhat Sahib*, the throne of temporal power, lies opposite Darbar Sahib.

Sri Darbar Sahib (Golden Temple), Amritsar

Everyone entering a gurdwara is expected to cover their head and remove any footwear. In

[11] Sain pronounced *"Saw-een"*

addition, tobacco, alcohol, or any other intoxicants are strictly forbidden on the gurdwara premises. Sikhs do not have any particular day for worship However, in North America and Europe the main service is typically held on Sundays or whatever day is a common holiday in the country in which they reside.

Sri Guru Granth Sahib is the primary focus of reverence in every gurdwara. It is placed on a *manji sahib* (an elevated platform) in the centre of the congregation hall (*darbar*). Seated behind the Sikh Scripture is a man or woman who periodically waves a large whisk (*chaur)* as a sign of respect for the Guru. Anyone from the congregation can perform this function. Devotees pay respect by bowing in front of the Scripture. People may donate money to meet the common needs of the institution and the community. Such donations are deposited in a large donation box (*golak*), placed in front, where they pay respect to

Sri Guru Singh Sabha, Surrey, BC

the Scripture. Donations are made on the basis of personal circumstances and are not prescribed.

Facing the *sangat* (congregation) is another elevated stage where *raagis* (devotional musicians) sing hymns from the Sri Guru Granth Sahib and lead the congregation in devotional singing. Sikhs do not have any ordained clergy. Instead, they have *gianis or granthis* - Sikhs who are learned in the Sikh Scripture, philosophy, and history. They act as caretakers of the Scripture and may fulfill this function as a full-time or part-time job. While any *amrithdari* (initiated) Sikh (man or woman) can perform the necessary services in the congregation, the gianis/granthis usually do so.

Sri Guru Singh Sabha, Surrey, BC

The congregation is seated on a carpeted floor, all as equals before the Guru. Frequently, men and women sit on separate sides, though there is no bar to them sitting together. It is felt that the separation of the sexes is conducive to meditation.

Everyone who enters the darbar hall, also called diwan hall, is given *karah-parshad*, a sweet pudding-like dish made out of flour, sugar, water, and butter. The karah-parshad is considered a blessing and is taken with open hands. It may be regarded as disrespectful or rude to decline the karah-parshad, and it is offensive to throw it away.

Every gurdwara has a *langar* hall (community kitchen), where food, usually prepared by volunteers, is served to all devotees and visitors alike throughout the day. Langar symbolizes equality and encourages the sharing of one's wealth and humility. It has deep roots in Sikh history. For example, the third Sikh Guru, Guru Amardas, declined to meet with the Mughal Emperor Akbar (1555-1605) until he sat on the floor and ate a meal with the commoners. The food in the langar is always vegetarian. The dishes are usually Punjabi food, though any ethnic vegetarian dish can be served in the langar. Generally, Sikhs will eat a meal after the end of the religious service, though it may be consumed at any time. Those that have limited financial means are encouraged to have langar, regardless of ethnicity, race, or religion.

Langar Hall

6. ARTICLES OF SIKH FAITH

In 1699 CE, Guru Gobind Singh created a distinctly separate Sikh identity, the *Khalsa*, through an initiation ceremony known as *Amrit*, which literally translates as "the nectar of immortality." It was an incredible mark of equality and humility when, after initiating the first five Sikhs (*panj pyare*), the Guru bowed before them and asked them to initiate him into the order. This gesture affirmed the belief in equality in Sikh religion and demonstrated that the disciple (Sikh) and the master (Guru) are equals in the eyes of the Divine.

Upon initiation, all Sikh women assume the surname *Kaur* (meaning lioness, Queen, or Sovereign), and men take on the surname *Singh* (meaning lion or King). A Sikh woman maintains her separate identity regardless of marriage and does not change her name to Singh. This naming process was a declaration that people of all backgrounds or castes were equal. The suffixes to their names, indicating their caste or status (according to the era's prevalent social practices) were replaced with the common last names of Kaur and Singh.

The use of last names other than Singh and Kaur is an artifact from the colonial era, where the British required Sikh men and women to take on additional last names as a way of identification. Frequently, these last names were taken from the names of the villages where they lived.

The Amrit *sanchar* (ceremony) is still practiced today, and the outward attire of modern-day practicing Sikhs (turban, unshorn hair, and other articles of faith) has been retained since Guru Gobind Singh's time.

The five *kakkars* (articles of faith – also referred to as the 5Ks), are an outward manifestation of Sikh beliefs and a core part of the Sikh identity. They have practical and spiritual significance and are more than symbols; they represent the values that guide a Sikh. These articles of faith are to be worn at all times, equally by men and women. The five kakkars and their significance are:

- **Kes** – unshorn hair, which represents the acceptance of God's will. *Kes* are to be kept covered at all times, with a *keski* or *dastaar* (turban). The turban [12] signifies humility, gender equality, and spiritual wisdom. Sikh women may wear a *keski* or other head covering, such as a scarf/dupatta.

- **Kangha** – is a wooden comb representing a sense of cleanliness and self-discipline. It is carried in the hair and used to keep the hair neat and tidy. As Sikhs comb their hair, they are also reminded to comb their mind of impurities and to detach themselves from material things.

[12] A poem written by Mohnaam Kaur, aged 11 years, describing the significance of the dastar (turban): *"I wear you every day; You give me the courage to stand up; You give me the confidence that I need; You give me the integrity to do what is right; You help my spiritual-self survive; You remind me to treat others equally; No matter who they might be; My humility comes from you; You are my identity."*

- **Kara** – is an iron or steel bracelet worn on  the dominant hand. The circle represents the continuum of the universe and the oneness of Waheguru. It serves to remind the bearer to follow Waheguru's command: to lead an honest, ethical, and compassionate life, to shed greed and ego, and to use one's hands for the benefit of humanity.

- **Kachhahira** – is a cotton undergarment that serves as a reminder to maintain high moral character and discipline. 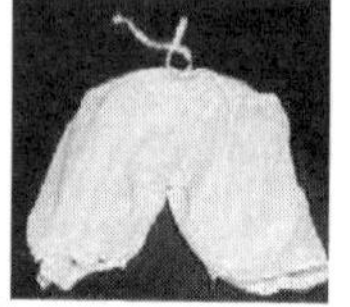

- **Kirpan** – a small sword, worn sheathed,  restrained in a cloth sash next to the body. The Kirpan is a composite word where *'Kirpa'* means grace or compassion, and *'aan'* means honour. The kirpan signifies the responsibility of a Sikh to stand up against injustice and assist those that are not able to advocate for themselves. It is a reminder to channel one's emotions towards positive ends, to act with compassion, rather than anger. The size of the kirpan worn varies depending on age and preference. It may range from as little as 1-3 inches for the young children and minimum of 6-9 inches for the adults.

7. SIKH CODE OF CONDUCT

Sikh religion is a practical, lived faith. Sikhs do not worship idols or practice religious rituals. Sikhs are expected to adhere to a simple code of conduct, known as the *Sikh Rehat Maryada,* which provides consistency and commonality of practices. The Sikh Rehat Maryada defines a Sikh as a person who faithfully believes in *"One Immortal Being, the Ten Gurus, the Sri Guru Granth Sahib, the teachings of the Gurus, and the Amrit initiation bequeathed by the tenth Guru. Furthermore, a Sikh is a person who does not owe allegiance to any other religion."*[13]

The *Sikh Rehat Maryada* sets out the basic requirements for Sikh worship and ceremonies to mark important life events, such as birth, initiation, marriage, and death. It also sets out some fundamental prohibitions, such as the consumption of intoxicants and substance abuse of any kind and refraining from cutting one's hair. Female infanticide, child marriage, and marriage

---

[13] Sikh Rehat Maryada (Sikh Code of Conduct), Section One – Translation from Punjabi version.

without the consent of the bride or groom are also strictly prohibited. Though most Sikhs are vegetarian, consumption of meat is not explicitly prohibited. The Sikh code of conduct prohibits eating *kutha,* meat of animal slaughtered through a painful or ritualistic manner.

The Sikh code of conduct is silent on issues such as birth control, abortion, euthanasia, artificial insemination, or in-vitro fertilization. However, deliberate miscarriage or abortion (unless the mother's health is judged to be in danger by competent medical practitioners), is considered taboo from a religious point of view, as it is an interference in the creative work of God. The Sikh faith also teaches us to respect the dignity and freedom of each person. We are, therefore, guided by our own conscious and interpretation of the teachings of the Gurus and are accountable for our actions, whether noble or immoral. "We are all judged by our deeds and actions," says Guru Nanak Sahib.[14] With that in mind, Sikhs, in general, are pro-choice on the issue of abortion.

---

14. SGGSp. 7: ਕਰਮੀ ਕਰਮੀ ਹੋਇ ਵੀਚਾਰੁ ॥

The attached Appendices “A,” “B,” “C,” and “D” describe the processes of naming a child, the Amrit (initiation), marriage, and death ceremonies, respectively.

8. COMMEMORATIONS

Sikhs do not believe that any particular day is holier than another. However, some historically significant events are publicly commemorated by Sikhs on the dates the events occurred.

- **Gurpurb:** Gurpurbs are days that mark the birth, martyrdom and joti jot anniversaries of the Sikh Gurus. On these days, Sikhs hold celebrations that include a full recitation of the Sri Guru Granth Sahib, followed by the singing of *kirtan* (also spelled keerten) or devotional Hymns, as well as appropriate lectures focusing on the historical significance of the occasion.
- **Sikh New Year:** Sikhs have their own calendar, called the *Nanakshahi* Calendar to mark special occasions. This calendar begins in the year 1469, which corresponds to the year that Guru Nanak, the founder of Sikh religion, was born. The Sikh New Year begins with the start of spring, in the month of Chet, which falls on March 14.

- **Hola Mohalla:** Hola Mohalla, or simply Hola, is a Sikh festival that is celebrated in March. The tradition was established by Guru Gobind Singh in the late seventeenth century to display and highlight Sikh martial arts through simulated battles. *Hola* means the onset of an attack or frontal assault, and *Mohalla* implies an organized procession in the form of an army column.

  Hola Mohalla is celebrated for three days in Anandpur Sahib, the city where Guru Gobind Singh held the first initiation ceremony for Sikhs. This festival draws millions of Sikhs and non-Sikhs from around the world.

- **Vaisakhi:** Vaisakhi occurs at the beginning of the month of Vaisakh - the second month in the Indian solar calendar (also called the *Bikrami Calendar)* and occurs around April 14 every year. Although Vaisakhi has traditionally been a harvest festival in Punjab and across South Asia for centuries, the day is particularly significant for Sikhs as it marks the initiation day of the Khalsa by Guru Gobind Singh in 1699 CE.

  Sikhs across the globe celebrate this seminal event through religious ceremonies in

Gurdwaras as well as public celebrations in the form of a *Nagar Kirtan.*

- **Nagar Kirtan:** A Nagar Kirtan is not an event, but rather a method of celebration. *Nagar* literally means a town, and *Kirtan refers* to the singing of devotional hymns. During a Nagar Kirtan, the participants sing hymns along public roads in the form of a celebratory march or parade. The procession is led by five *amritdhari* (initiated) Sikhs (panj payare), followed by the Sri Guru Granth Sahib installed in a decorated float. The celebrations are open to all members of the public and include public displays of *gatka* (Sikh martial arts) as well as floats depicting historical or social themes. Along the parade route, people set up tents and offer free food and beverages to all attendees.
- **Ghallughara Akal Takhat Sahib (1984):** The first week of June is commemorated as Ghallughara (holocaust) day. During this week, in 1984, thousands of innocent Sikh pilgrims and families, including young children, were massacred by the Indian Army during their attack on the Darbar Sahib (Golden Temple) complex and thirty-eight other historical Gurdwaras in Punjab. The assault was code-

named *"Operation Blue Star"* by the Indian Government.

- **Sikh Genocide Week (1984):** The Sikh community commemorates the first week of November as *'Sikh Genocide Week'* to remember the November 1984 pogrom during which over 14,000[15] Sikhs were killed in a systematic and orchestrated attack following the murder of Prime Minister Indira Gandhi by her two Sikh bodyguards. Sikhs were killed in horrific ways, many burnt alive with rubber tires around their necks, and women and girls' gang-raped in front of their family members before being tortured and killed.
- **Bandi Chhod Divas:** The *Bandi Chhod Divas* (Day of Liberation) is a Sikh celebratory day which coincides with Diwali, the Indian festival of lights. On this day, Sikhs commemorate the release of the sixth guru, Guru Hargobind, from years of unlawful imprisonment at the Gwalior Fort by the Mughal Emperor Jahangir.

---

[15] The office death toll by the Government of India is 3,000. However, independent human rights groups put the toll at almost five times that number.

History has it that when he was finally offered his release, Guru Hargobind refused to leave the prison unless all 52 Hindu princes, who were rulers of the mountainous regions of Punjab and had also been wrongfully imprisoned, were released. Emperor Jahangir agreed, but with a caveat: he would only allow the release of prisoners who could hold onto the corners of the Guru's robe. Guru Hargobind wisely designed a robe tailored with 52 "corners" or strings, forcing Jahangir to let him depart with all fifty-two rulers trailing behind him, each holding a "corner" of the robe. This day is celebrated by Sikhs every November.

CONCLUSION

A Sikh is a student who embarks on an internal journey to seek the truth about their true existence, and about their relationship with the Creator, the universe, and others. A Sikh endeavours to see the presence of Divine light in everyone and everything around them. Divine presence can be readily experienced when one practices the principles of righteous living.

Guru Nanak emphasized a three-pronged approach to life, emphasizing a practical commitment to balance the spiritual quest with one's obligations to family and society at large:

- Earning one's livelihood through honest means (*kirat karna*);
- Embarking on a quest for internal purity through meditation (*naam japna*); and
- Sharing one's earnings with others, particularly the needy (*vand chhakna*).

For a Sikh, *Waheguru*, the formless Divine Creator is omnipresent, and everyone, irrespective of religious beliefs, gender, sexual orientation, race, ethnicity, geographic origins, or linguistic background, can readily connect with the Creator without needing an intermediary or resorting to customary rituals.

A Sikh considers prayer and meditation as ways of directly communicating with the Divine, which can be silent, spoken, or sung through hymns. This communication can be performed individually in private, or collectively as part of a congregation. The Sikh *Ardas* (prayer) marking the commencement or conclusion of an event, concludes with a request to the Divine to bless all of humanity *(Sarbat da bhala),* and not just a chosen few.

The five articles of the Sikh faith (5Ks) comprise the physical manifestation of the Sikh identity. They have practical and spiritual significance and therefore are not mere symbols. These five articles represent the values that constitute the foundations of the Sikh faith and are to be worn by all Sikhs at all times. Superstitions or idol worship are antithetical to Sikh values.

Guru Nanak maintained that all religions are equal and sought to unify people of different faiths rather than divide them. He introduced a new approach to life and encouraged self-awareness and truthful living. Two of the most significant elements of Guru Nanak's vision were his dedication to women's rights and casteless society. In Sikhism, women are equal to men in their role, status, and power. Racism, sexism, or religious superiority have no place in Sikh faith.

There is a *sakhi* (story) about Guru Nanak encountering a village during his travels, where the residents were rude and inhospitable. Upon leaving the village, the Guru blessed them by saying, *"vasdey raho"* (may you prosper and stay here forever). In the next village, the residents were kind and welcoming. The Guru's departing words to them were *"ujhar jao"* (may you be displaced). Upon hearing these words, Guru Nanak's travelling companion, Mardana, asked him why he would give such counterintuitive blessings to the residents of each village. Guru Nanak cxplained that the inhabitants of the first village had such undesirable habits that it was better that they stayed put and did not spread their negative thinking elsewhere. But in the second village, the personal qualities of the residents were such that the Guru hoped they would disperse and spread their goodwill to others.

The Sikhs have taken Guru Nanak's advice to heart and have spread from Punjab to every continent of the world. Rare is a country that does not have some Sikh residents. And yet, Sikhism is not a proselytizing faith. Instead, the focus for a Sikh is to live a life of inward reflection, which informs outward action. In that way, Sikhs strive to create a just and fair society, where all may worship and live in their own unique ways, all the while flourishing and growing together.

APPENDIX "A"

Naam Sanskar (Naming Ceremony)

Whether the child is born at home or in the hospital, soon as the mother and child are physically able, or released from the hospital, the family travels to the Gurdwara and performs the *Naam Sanskaar* or naming ceremony.

Once inside the Gurdwara, the *Giani/Granthi* (Curator and scripture reader) will recite or sing a verse from the Sikh Scripture *"Satgur Sache Diya Bhej"* – Thank you, Waheguru, for blessing the family with a child,"[16] and do an *Ardas* (prayer) seeking Guru's blessings to name the newborn. Then Sri Guru Granth Sahib is opened at random, and the first Sabd (hymn) to appear on the top left-hand corner is recited. It is called *Hukam* or *Vak* (divine directive). The name of the child is selected by choosing a name that starts with the first letter of the first word of the *Sabd.*

---

[16] SGGSp.396: "ਸਤਿਗੁਰ ਸਾਚੈ ਦੀਆ ਭੇਜਿ ॥ .."

Regardless of what name is selected, all Sikh names must be given a suffix - *'Singh'* meaning lion for the boys and *'Kaur'* meaning princess or royalty for the girls. The tenth Guru initiated this practice to emphasize equality and to break caste and social barriers. After the naming ceremony, *Karah-parshad* is distributed.

APPENDIX "B"

Amrit Sanskar (Initiation Ceremony)

On Vaisakhi day in 1699 CE, in a massive gathering of over 80,000 in Anandpur Sahib, Punjab, Guru Gobind Singh unsheathed his sword and asked if someone was willing to sacrifice themself. The *Sangat* (congregation) went numb. After a brief pin drop silence, five Sikhs successively came forward. The Guru held a unique initiation ceremony, called *Amrit Sanchar* or *Khande Di Pahul,* and declared the five to be the first *Panj Pyare* (five beloveds). He added the suffix Singh to their names, and *Bhai* means brother (Bhai Daya Singh, Bhai Dharam Singh, Bhai Himat Singh, Bhai Mohkam Singh, and Bhai Sahib Singh), and then knelt before them to request they initiate him. He also changed his name from Gobind Rai to Gobind Singh. Thus, the Guru created an institution of loyal Sikhs, called the Khalsa (pure, sovereign), who were bound by common identity and discipline.

Sikhs aspiring to join the Khalsa fraternity go through the *Amrit ceremony* similar to the one administered by Guru Gobind Singh. It provides an opportunity for the Sikhs of any time period, and in any country or place, to give themselves to the spiritual light of the Guru in a complete and absolute way. Those who accept *Amrit* commit to becoming protectors and custodians of the Universal Truths contained within the Sri Guru Granth Sahib and of all living beings. They practice the spiritual way of life that the Sikh Gurus taught and modelled. By taking Amrit, one surrenders one's body, mind, and wealth (*Tan, Man, and Dhan*), and dedicates to preserving the Sikh tradition and wisdom, and uplifting humanity.

The Amrit ceremony usually takes place in a Gurdwara. It is presided over by the *Panj Pyare* (five Khalsas), who represent the first five Beloved Ones who gave their heads to Guru Gobind Singh. All candidates for initiation gather together in the Gurdwara or any other designated place, where Sri Guru Granth Sahib is present.

The ceremony starts with an Ardas. All candidates arrive wearing five articles of faith (explained in chapter 6). They sit cross-legged and meditate in unison with the Panj Pyare. Each one of the Panj Pyare takes a turn to recite one of the five *Banis*, select spiritual utterances of the Gurus *(Jap, Jaap, Chaupaee, Tav Prasad Savaiye, and Anand)* that are part of a Khalsa's daily meditation routine. Concurrently, they prepare Amrit (Nectar) by churning *patase* (sugar puffs) and water in an iron bowl, using a *Khanda* (double-edged sword). This process takes between 2-4 hours, depending upon the number of people seeking Amrit.

The candidates then come forward to receive Amrit and participate in a beautiful and powerful ceremony of transformation. Everyone drinks the *Amrit* from the same bowl, accepting the equality of all, irrespective of their background and social status. The Amrit Sanskar/Sanchar ceremony opens the door for the initiated Sikhs to manifest their purity and light in every aspect of their future lives.

An initiated Sikh is called "Amritdhari" or "Khalsa." Henceforth, their names are suffixed Singh (male) or Kaur (female). They commit to the following obligations:

- carry all five articles of faith with them all the times (including when they shower and go to bed).
- meditate daily on the same five *banis* (divine utterances) that are recited at the time of preparing Amrit.
- refrain from four transgressions: dishonoring hair, eating meat (*kutha*), [17] adultery, and using tobacco, alcohol or other intoxicating substances.

---

[17] In Sikh Rehat Maryada, the word kutha means meat of an animal slaughtered in the Muslim way.

APPENDIX "C"

Anand Sanskar (Marriage Ceremony)

Sikh marriage is called *Anand Karj*, which roughly translates to a mystical experience, spiritual bliss, or a state of happiness.

Sikhs do not believe in living a monastic life. Marriage is celebrated. As humans, we constantly search for happiness and fulfillment. A critical step towards accomplishing this goal is through marriage, which brings together two souls in a spiritual union. *"Merely sitting together does not make them husband and wife. Instead, henceforth they must become ONE - make all decisions jointly, acting like one soul in two bodies and contemplate on Waheguru (God),"* says, Guru Amardas.[18]

There are many reasons why people may choose to get married, whether it is for emotional gratification, economic security, legal legitimacy, or social acceptance. Marriage for Sikhs, however, far exceeds these bounds. Marriage is seen as an integral part of the spiritual experience, where the

---

[18] SGGSp.788: "Ek Jot Doay Murti" - ਏਕ ਜੋਤਿ ਦੁਇ ਮੂਰਤੀ ॥ "

married couple embarks on a journey together towards self-discovery and community service. Guru Arjan, the fifth guru, says that *"the family life is an asset and an enjoinder to a couple's faith."*[19]

A Sikh couple wanting to get married comes to the Gurdwara and presents themselves before the Sri Guru Granth Sahib for spiritual guidance. It is this part of the human journey that leads them to self-discovery and guides them to understand who they are and what their purpose is in life.

As previously stated, Sikhs do not have a class of clergy or priests. A Giani, or for that matter any *Amritdhari* (initiated) Sikh, man or woman, who is familiar with the responsibilities of conducting marriages, can perform the wedding rite. The Sikh Code of Conduct (*Sikh Rehat Maryada*) Section XVIII explains the process of solemnizing a marriage.

The essence of the Anand Karj ceremony: The connection with the Guru, with each other and the community at large, starts with a silent prayer led by the Giani/Granthi, while the bride,

---

[19] SGGS71: "girastee girasat dharmaataa-ਗਿਰਸਤੀ ਗਿਰਸਤਿ ਧਰਮਾਤਾ ॥ "

groom, and their parents stand with folded hands in prayer. The rest of the *sangat* (congregation) remain seated. However, if a family so desires, the whole congregation may stand and join in prayer.

A *vak,* also called *hukam* (divine directive for the event), follows the prayer. The Giani/Granthi randomly selects a verse from the Sri Guru Granth Sahib by opening the Scripture and reading the stanza, which appears on the top left-hand corner of the open page in the Scripture. The vak is read out loud and is regarded as the blessing to the couple as they begin the marriage ceremony.

The next step in the ceremony is called the *palla* (a kind of ceremonial shawl) ceremony. The bride's parent or guardian takes one end of the *palla* from around the groom's shoulders and hands it to the bride, while the groom grasps the other end of the palla. This symbolizes the commencement of their union. While this is happening, the *kirtan jatha* (devotional musicians) sing the following hymn, *"O Waheguru, all relationships are false and tough to shoulder; hence we have jointly grasped the hem of your robe and implore your blessing."*[20]

[20] SGGSp.963: "ਹਭੇ ਸਾਕ ਕੂੜਾਵੇ ਡਿਠੈ ਤਉ ਪਲੈ ਤੈਡੈ ਲਾਗੀ ॥ "

The central part of the marriage ceremony then begins, where the four wedding vows (*lavan* – *lav* (ਲਾਵ) singular and *lavan* (ਲਾਵਾਂ) plural) are read and sung in succession, as the bride and groom walk around the Scripture.

The lavan are prescribed in the Sri Guru Granth Sahib (SGGS, pp.773-774). The words are intended to guide the couple on how to maneuver through their married life together and how to grow and connect with the Divine. As a Giani/Granthi recites the first lav, the couple stands with folded hands and listens attentively. At the end of the recitation, the couple bows down, and gets up together to walk in a circle around the Sri Guru Granth Sahib, in a clockwise direction. During this time, the Kirtan jatha sings the same lav. Though the order is not prescribed religiously, it has become customary for the groom to walk ahead of the bride.

By walking around the Sri Guru Granth Sahib, the couple asserts their agreement to the marriage and to abide by the words of the Guru. Sometimes a bride may wish to walk the circle while aided by her male relatives. This practice is discouraged as it goes against the Sikh values of gender equality and free will.

At the end of the first lav, the couple bows in unison, kneeling and touching their forehead to the floor with respect, meaning, "Yes, I accept this commitment." The reading of the second lav begins, and the same steps are repeated four times.

The four lavan, or vows, represent the four stages of spiritual growth as well as growth in the relationship. They translate loosely to the following:

- **First Lav** – In the first lav, the couple commits to letting go of the past and embarking on a new journey together. The lav sets out the daily duties of married life. It emphasizes their obligations towards themselves, each other, their families, the community, and humanity at large. Social responsibilities are to be fulfilled with integrity and compassion and are to be informed by the spiritual teachings of the Sri Guru Granth Sahib.

- **Second Lav** – The second lav conveys the strengthening of their emotional bond. As they each fulfill their social duties with integrity, the couple begins to develop respect for each other, and their love for each other deepens. They commit to putting aside their ego and other materialistic attachment and replacing it with a desire for internal peace through the singing of Waheguru's praises.

- **Third Lav** – The third lav signifies the couple's detachment from the past and their profound desire to never be apart from each other and to join with Waheguru (God) as one.

- **Fourth Lav** – The final lav describes the state of harmony and union experienced in married life during which human love blends into the love of the divine.

At the conclusion of the fourth lav, the marriage ceremony is completed. The Kirtan Jatha sing the Anand Sahib – song of bliss, following which a congregational prayer is held where all rise as the Giani leads the congregation in ardas (prayer).

A vak is again taken from the Sri Guru

Granth Sahib and becomes the Guru's message to the married couple as they embark on their life together as a married couple. *Karah-prashad* is handed out to everyone. While it is not a religious requirement, some countries including Canada require the couple to sign the marriage register maintained by a Giani or an authorized executive member of the Gurdwara. This is done after the karah-prashad has been handed out.

APPENDIX "D"

Antam Sanskar (Funeral Ceremony)

Sikhs accept death as the fulfillment of their journey on earth and an opportunity to merge into Divine light. How the body is disposed of makes no difference to the dead. Cremation is the preferred method of disposal and is recommended by the Sikh Code of Conduct. However, when cremation is not a practical option, the remains may be immersed in running water, donated to scientific research organizations, or disposed of appropriately by whatever suitable means available according to the extenuating circumstances. Cremation is considered the most natural way of decomposing the body and is economical and environmentally safe, compared to burial.

The Sikh Code of Conduct outlines certain religious rites that Sikhs must follow when someone passes away. The body is washed and dressed up in fresh clothes before cremation. If the deceased person was A*mritdhari*, they must be donned with all five articles of faith (see explanation in chapter 6). In India, the cremation usually takes place the same day as the death, unless there are extenuating circumstances to wait for close relatives. A prayer is done at the time of the funeral, and subsequently, a *Sehaj Path or Akhand Path* (reading of Sikh Scripture) is started, and a final prayer is done on completion of the reading.

In North America, irrespective of where the death occurs, the body is sent to the crematorium, and the cremation is arranged to accommodate the availability of relatives to attend. In the United Kingdom, the Sikhs follow a slightly different custom. On the day of cremation, they bring the body home for a prayer and then to the Gurdwara for public viewing, and finally to the crematorium for public viewing and cremation. Due to limited crematorium availability in the Western hemisphere, it takes longer to find a spot for cremation. As such, the *Sehaj Path* is started on the day of death and completed with a final prayer on the day of cremation.

Some Sikhs take the ashes to Kiratpur Sahib,[21] Punjab, and dispose of them in the river there. This is not a requirement. Sikhs are recommended to dispose of the ashes in running water anywhere, and if that is not possible, they can bury them anywhere, including in their backyards.

[21] The town was established by Sri Guru Hargobind Sahib in 1627 CE. It is situated on the bank of the Satluj river. Sri Guru Har Rai Sahib and Sri Guru Harkrishan Sahib were born here.

ACKNOWLEDGEMENT

Thank you, Waheguru, for your blessings and for guiding me through the process of writing this book. It is always a challenge to write about religion, and this book was no different. My task was made much easier by academic reviews by Dr. Balwant Singh Dhillon, former Dean, Professor and founding director of Sri Guru Granth Sahib studies at Guru Nanak Dev University (GNDU), Amritsar, who also wrote an insightful foreword, and Dr. Gurnam Singh Sanghera, a former principal and visiting professor at the Centre for Studies on Sri Guru Granth Sahib, at GNDU. I sincerely appreciate their scholarly advice.

It was a bonus to have Dr. Dharam Singh and Dr. Paramvir Singh, former and current head, respectively, of the '*Encyclopedia* of *Sikhism*' Punjabi University, Patiala, for their review and prized suggestions.

I am genuinely grateful to my wife, Surinder Kaur, for being a true partner in everything undertake. She is my resource library for *Sabd* (hymn) references when needed. I owe a bundle of gratitude and love to my grandchildren (Mohnaam Kaur, Kurbaan Singh, and Eimaan Singh) to review the draft and provide valuable input, and Manraj Kaur for her creative and artistic cover page design.

No book is ever complete without the piercing eye of an editor. For that, I am grateful to my dear friend Guy Saady, who provided objective feedback to make the book more reader friendly.

Gian Singh Sandhu

SELECTED GLOSSARY OF PUNJABI TERMS

Aad Granth	The premier Sikh Scripture
Akal Takhat	A seat of Sikh temporal authority in Amritsar (literally, the Throne of the Timeless One)
Amrit	The nectar of immortality, prepared for initiating the Sikhs
Amritdhari	A person who has been initiated into the Sikh faith and abides by the Sikh code of conduct, including carrying all articles of faith at all times
Amrit Sanchar	Initiation ceremony – also called Khande Di Pahul
Anand	Spiritual bliss
Anand Karj	Sikh marriage rites – spiritual bliss or union
Ardas	Prayer, request, petition, supplication
Baba	Grandfather, or wise elder, it is an honorific used to refer to someone who is deeply respected for their knowledge and leadership, regardless of their age. The female term is *Bibi*
Bandi	Imprisoned
Bandi Chhod	Liberator
Bandi Chhod Divas	Day of liberation
Bhai	Brother
Chaur	A ceremonial whisk waved over the Sikh Scripture
CE	Common Era
Darbar	Congregation hall
Darbar Hall	Main congregation hall in a Gurdwara
Darbar Sahib	Most revered place of worship for the Sikhs. Also known as the Harimandir Sahib

Dastar	Turban
Divas	Day, celebration day
Giani / Granthi	Sikh Scripture reader, who is well versed with Sikh philosophy, and history. They must be Amritdhari
Golak	A receptacle in which offerings made to the Guru are kept
Gurdwara	Sikh place of congregation and worship
Gurmukhi	Punjabi script standardized by Guru Angad
Gurpurb	Celebration of Sikh Gurus' anniversaries
Guru	Deliverer or liberator from darkness (ignorance) to light (enlightenment).
Guru Granth Sahib	The Sikh Scripture, the final and Eternal Guru of the Sikhs
Hola Mohalla	A Sikh festival which follows the Holi festival
Hukam/Vak	A hymn from the scripture opened at random. It is taken as Guru's command
Janamsakhi	A hagiographical account of Guru's life
Janeu	A sacred religious thread worn by Hindu men
Jatha	Hymn singing group, or an assembled group, often for a particular purpose.
Ji	Suffix connoting respect
Kachhahira	Cotton undergarment, one of five articles of the Sikh faith
Kakkars	Sikh articles of faith
Kangha	Wooden comb, one of five articles of the Sikh faith
Kara	Iron bracelet, one of five articles of the Sikh faith
Kaur	Princess/royalty

Kes	Uncut hair, one of five articles of the Sikh faith that must be covered with a turban
Kirtan	The singing of scriptural hymns
Khalsa	An initiated Sikh who abides by the Sikh Rehat Maryada, the Sikh code of conduct
Khalsa Panth	The collective body of initiated adherents of the Sikh faith
Kirpan	Sword, one of Five Ks
Kirt Karna	Earning an honest living
Langar	Community kitchen in a Gurdwara, where everyone sits on the floor and eats together irrespective of their social status.
Lav	Sikh matrimony vow (single)
Lavan	Plural lav
Manji Sahib	An elevated platform
Miri	Temporal power or sovereignty
Misl	A small, independent principality
Mool Mantar	Lit. creedal formula, recorded in the beginning of Guru Granth Sahib
Nagar	Town
Nagar Kirtan	Sikh procession singing hymns on public roads. Sometimes referred to as Parade
Naam Japna	Remembrance of Name Divine
Nishan Sahib	Sikh flag
Panj Pyare	Five beloved Amritdhari (initiated) Sikhs
Panth	A term used in Sikh tradition for the Sikhs as a whole

Parshad	A sweet pudding-like dish made out of flour, sugar, water, and butter – served to all who enter the gurdwara
Patase	Sugar puffs
Piri	Spiritual sovereignty
Raag	Musical measures/modes
Raagi	Sikh hymn singer, musicians
Rehat Maryada	Sikh code of conduct
Saka	A heroic historical event
Sanchar	Ceremony
Sangat	Congregation present in a Gurdwara
Sarb-sanjha	All inclusive, accessible to all
Sati	The Hindu ritual of burning a widow on her husband's funeral pyre
SGGS	Sri Guru Granth Sahib, the Sikh Scripture.
SGPC	Shiromani Gurdwara Parbandhak Committee
Singh	Lion (denoting initiated Sikh male)
Sri	Prefix used as a sign of reverence or respect
Tan, Man, Dhan	Body, mind and wealth
Vak	A randomly opened hymn from the Sikh Scripture. It is considered as the Divine directive for the event
Vaisakhi	The founding of the Khalsa, and the first day of the month of Vaisakh, celebrated annually by the Sikhs around the world.
Vand Chhakna	Sharing of one's earning with others, particularly the needy
Waheguru	God, Divine or Creator, also spelled as Vahiguru in the western hemisphere

Bibliography and Further Reading

Cunningham, J.D – "The History of Sikhs," 1990 reprint 1994, DK Publishers New Delhi

Cole, Owen W – "Understanding Sikhism," 2004, Dunedin Academic Press

Dhillon, Balwant Singh Dr.: "Early Sikh Scriptural Traditions" 1999, Singh Brothers, Amritsar, India.

Greenlees, Duncan – "The Gospel of the Guru Granth Sahib" – 1975 The Theological Publishing House, London

Kaur, Madanjit **Dr.**- "Guru Gobind Singh and Creation of Khalsa, 2000, Guru Nanak Dev University, Amritsar.

Khalsa, Sant Singh Dr. – "Sri Guru Granth Sahib" English Translation.

Mansukhani, Gobind Singh – "Sikh Ethics" www.allaboutsikhs.com

Rahi, Malkiat Singh – "Guru Granth Sahib in the Eyes of Non-Sikh Scholars," 2003, Singh Legal Foundation, Chandigarh

Sandhu, Gian Singh – "An Uncommon Road" – How Canadian Sikhs struggled out of the fringes and into the mainstream (2018) – Echo Story Telling, Vancouver, BC.

Sikh Rehat Maryada - (Code of Conduct) – English and Punjabi versions available in print and online on google.

Singh Avtar: "ETHICS OF THE SIKHS," 2009, Publication Bureau, Punjabi University, Patiala

Singh, Baldev Ph.D.: "GURMAT - Guru Nanak's Path of Enlightenment, 2015, Published by Hardev Singh Shergill

Singh, Dharam: "GURU NANAK – Contemporary Concerns and Response" (2019), Singh Brothers, Amritsar

Singh, I.J. "The Sikhs Today." Ideas and Opinions, (2012). Ethinicisland.com

Singh, Jagjit - "The Sikhism," Culture, History and Religion" – 2008, Chattar Singh Jeevan Singh

Singh, Khushwant – "A History of the Sikhs" Volume 1, 1469-1838 & Volume 2, 1839-2004 Oxford University Press, 2004,

Singh, Manmohan Dr. – "Sri Guru Granth Sahib," English Translation.

Singh, Nikki Guninder Kaur – "Sikhism: An Introduction to Religion," 2011, IB Tauris

Singh, Ranbir – "The Sikh Way of Life"–India Publishers 3rd Edition 1982.

Singh, Sahib Prof. "Sri Guru Granth Sahib (Sikh Spiritual Writings) Darpan, in Punjabi.

Toynbee, Arnold – "Selections from the Sacred Writings of the Sikhs," 1960 UNESCO Book

Tuli, Pritpal Singh – "Sikh Traditions and Festivals" – 2013, Chattar Singh Jiwan Singh, Amritsar

Websites:

- **Sikh Feminist Research Institute:** www.sikhfeministresearch.org
- **Sikh National Archives of Canada:** www.sikhnationalarchives.com
- **Sikh Net** www.sikhnet.com
- **Sikh Research Institute** www.sikhri.org
- **World Sikh Organization of Canada** www.worldsikh.org